Watch for these titles coming up in the
Choose Your Own Adventure® series.

Ask your bookseller for books you have missed
or visit us at cyoa.com to learn more.

THE CASE OF THE SILK KING

BY SHANNON GILLIGAN

INTERIOR ILLUSTRATION BY
V. PORNKERD, S. YAWEERA, & J. DONPLOYPETCH
COVER ILLUSTRATION BY JOSE LUIS MARRON

CHOOSE YOUR OWN ADVENTURE® CLASSICS
A DIVISION OF

CHOOSECO
WAITSFIELD, VERMONT

The Case of the Silk King ©1986 R. A. Montgomery,
Warren, Vermont. All Rights Reserved

Artwork, design, and revised text ©2005 Chooseco LLC,
Waitsfield, Vermont. All Rights Reserved

Interior illustrated by: V. Pornkerd, S. Yaweera, & J. Donploypetch
Cover Illusration by: Jose Luis Marron
Book design: Stacey Hood, Big Eyedea Visual Design
Chooseco dragon logos designed by: Suzanne Nugent

For information regarding permission, write to:

CHOOSECO
P.O. Box 46
Waitsfield, Vermont 05673
www.cyoa.com

ISBN 10 1-933390-14-X
ISBN 13 978-1-933390-14-7

Published simultaneously in the United States and Canada

Printed in the United States

0 9 8 7 6 5

*For my Aunt Nui
and Uncle Snoh,
with much love
—SG*

AUTHOR'S NOTE

Jim Thompson was an American OSS officer stationed in Thailand at the end of the second World War. He stayed on in Thailand after the war to develop a silk manufacturing and export business. This silk business became a terrific success. Over Easter weekend 1967, while visiting close friends Helen and T. G. Ling, Thompson disappeared mysteriously. These are the facts.

All other persons and events in this book are the product of my imagination and are entirely fictitious. Any relation to persons living or dead, or to actual occurrences, is purely coincidental.

BEWARE and WARNING!

This book is different from other books.

You and YOU ALONE are in charge of what happens in this story.

There are dangers, choices, adventures and consequences. YOU must use all of your wits and much of your exceptional intelligence. The wrong decision could end in disaster—even death. But, don't despair. At anytime, YOU can go back and make another choice, alter the path of your story, and change its result.

The year is 1982 and an anonymous package arrives in the mail. It contains a clipping from the Bangkok Post, a plane ticket to Thailand and $2000 to help in your search for a man who disappeared without a trace. The only problem was that he was last seen 15 years ago. Could he still be alive? Should you travel to Thailand to find out?

It's March 26, 1982.

You sit at your desk reading the morning papers. You keep up with the news because you find current events fascinating, but it's also important in your work. An uninformed detective, especially with international cases, is hardly a good detective. You note that President Ronald Reagan has made a strong statement about the recent Russian offensive in Afghanistan. As you browse through the paper, you see an article "Fifteenth Anniversary of the Disappearance of the Silk King." There aren't many kings left in the world and that's one you hadn't heard of.

Pling!

You look up as the screen door snaps. It's Sam, your secretary, carrying several pieces of mail.

Turn to page 2.

"Anything interesting?" you ask.

"Just this," he replies, handing you a plain brown envelope. You look the envelope over. The address of your detective agency has been neatly typed out.

"Hmm, that's odd," you say. "There's no return address."

Whatever is inside, you hope it's about a new case. It's been almost a year and a half since you solved the case of the missing tea bowl and uncovered a Japanese Mafia ring. That case received international attention. So when you and your folks moved back to the States, you had no problem getting detective work. But lately things have been pretty slow. The highlight of your summer so far has been finding a lost cat.

"Holy crow!" Sam exclaims as you rip open the envelope. Two one-thousand-dollar bills, a plane ticket, and a newspaper article flutter slowly to your desk.

"It looks like a job to me," you say, smiling.

"And I think it has something to do with this," Sam says, picking up the article.

Go on to the next page.

Sam peers over your shoulder as you read the newspaper article. It tells an incredible story about the disappearance of a man named Jim Thompson, sometimes known as the Thai Silk King. You glance back at your paper. So that's the "king." What a coincidence that you were reading that very article just as Sam came in with the letter. It's almost like an omen. You wonder if it's a good one or a bad one. You read on.

Thompson was an American OSS agent who stayed on in Thailand at the end of the Second World War. He started a silk-weaving business that grew wildly, far beyond anyone's expectations. In his spare time, Thompson amassed an outstanding collection of Asian art and built a Thai-style house to put it in. He had many friends and entertained frequently.

In fact, Jim Thompson led a seemingly charmed life until one fateful day in March 1967. He was vacationing over Easter with friends in the Cameron Highlands in Malaysia when he suddenly disappeared without a trace. Despite an intensive search involving hundreds of volunteers, not a single clue was ever found.

Then, last week, two photos of a small Thai village market arrived at the offices of the Bangkok Post in an envelope with no return address. The envelope was postmarked the first of March. It was from Sisaket, a Thai city close to the Cambodian border.

Turn to page 4.

4

In the background of both photos was an elderly Caucasian man dressed like a Buddhist monk. The paper's editor noticed that this man looked like Thompson and invited several people who had known Jim Thompson well to look at the pictures. Despite the fact that Thompson had been declared legally dead by a Thai court in 1974, everyone who saw the photos felt sure that the monk was none other than Thompson himself!

Thompson's friends have offered a $100,000 reward for any further information leading to his recovery, and the photos have been placed on display in the offices of the Bangkok Post.

Turn to page 9.

"I can't leave for Bangkok before I research the case," you tell Sam. "And besides I have to find out who's sending me on this trip. I don't like the idea of an invisible client."

"I guess you're right," Sam agrees.

"I want you to take this entire package down to Sergeant Wimble and ask him to run a fingerprint scan on all of it, even the money. If you find out anything, I'll be at the library researching the newspaper reports on Thompson's disappearance."

"Right," Sam says, darting out the door with the mystery envelope in hand.

An hour later, you are down in the cool, quiet stacks of the library, flipping through copies of the Washington Post from Spring 1967. There are plenty of articles on Thompson. You read in detail about his disappearance and the search afterward. As the search begins to appear hopeless, the newspaper stories start to introduce various kidnap theories. And it is from one of these articles in mid-April that a whole section has been neatly cut out.

You quickly check the edition of the New York Times for the same day. A section is missing from the Thompson article in that paper, too!

Turn to page 16.

When you wake up, you're in a monastery someplace. Your head will be fine, but your memory is blank. The crack on your skull has given you a bad case of amnesia. You have no idea who you are, where you're from, or why you're here. Your passport and all other identifying papers were lost when your pack was carried away by the flood waters.

Other flood victims are at the monastery, being nursed by the monks. Gradually, the other victims recover and return to their homes. You remain at the monastery, however. In truth, the officials are not sure what to do with you, and it seems the best place to keep you for the time being.

Gradually you fall into the simple ascetic routine of the monks and nuns around you. After six months, you decide to become a member of this Buddhist community.

You lead a long, fulfilling life of good works. Many years later, someone tells you the story of a legendary American monk. He, too, was discovered injured and was nursed back to health by Buddhist monks. He, too, on his recovery joined the ranks of the monastery. He worked hard among the people and served the Thai nation selflessly. His name was Jim Thompson.

The End

8

You pass by the branch trail as you continue along the trail you've been following. For now, it's enough just to cover the marked trails well. You'll have the chance to bushwhack tomorrow.

At first it's hard to tell anything apart as everything is green. Gradually you begin to make out different plants, and to pick out the trees from the bushes, but it's not easy. Some bushes are as big as the trees back home.

You come to a large forked tree covered with tiny wild orchids. Wait! Didn't you pass this tree a while back? You look at the map. According to your calculations, you're a short way from a crossroads. From there you can take a path back to town.

Half an hour later, you're still walking. The crossroads is nowhere in sight. What's worse, everything begins to look familiar. When you pass the tree with the wild orchids again, you know you're definitely walking in circles.

You remember Major Kaye's remark about instructions on the bottom of the map if you are lost. You find the list of rules and start reading.

Turn to page 10.

"What a strange story!" Sam exclaims.

"Yes, especially that part about Thompson being in the OSS," you add.

"What's the OSS?" Sam asks.

"It stands for Office of Strategic Services," you reply. "Later it turned into the CIA."

"You mean Thompson was once a spy?"

"Probably. And you know what they say: Once a spy, always a spy."

"Maybe he was rubbed out by old enemies!" Sam suggests.

"One thing's for sure. I'll have to find out more about Jim Thompson before I leave."

"You won't have time if you're planning to use this ticket," Sam says. "Your flight leaves for Bangkok tonight."

"Tonight?" you ask incredulously, reaching for the ticket. "But I hardly know anything about the case. Or who's sending me. Or why!"

"Yes, but six days have already passed since the photos were identified," Sam reminds you. "If you don't leave now, you may never have a chance at that reward."

If you decide to leave for Bangkok tonight, turn to page 15.

If you decide to put off leaving until you have more information, turn to page 6.

Hints to Walkers

If you are lost : walk due east or west, whichever is opposite to the way you came. Eventually you will come to the main road.

If you are uncertain as to the direction of east or west, stay where you are, if possible near a stream, until you are found. This may take twenty-four hours.

DO NOT PANIC.
KEEP TO THE NUMBERED TRAILS.

You look up. The tiny patches of sky visible through the trees are sullen and gray. It's impossible to tell east from west. That means you should wait right where you are. But can you stand just waiting? You're not sure. Searches take a long time. You haven't eaten since last night; you're starved and you're lost. You look again at the sign that says

Go on to the next page.

"DO NOT PANIC." You take a deep breath, but you know you have to make a decision now.

Then you remember the two smoke bombs in your pocket. Maybe you should set one off?

If you decide to follow the map instructions and stay where you are, turn to page 49.

If you decide to keep walking and try one last time to find your way back, turn to page 13.

If you decide to set off a smoke bomb, turn to page 41.

"Thompson normally enjoyed trips like that. But he seemed peculiarly restless this time," Mr. Sing answers. "He insisted on returning early. When they got back, they all decided to take naps. But when the other three woke up, Thompson was gone."

"Lost on a walk in the jungle?" you ask.

"I myself favor the idea that Jim was kidnapped," Mr. Sing answers and ticks off a long list of kidnap motives.

You begin to feel dizzy. Straight lines seem to waver, and you have trouble focusing.

"Excusth me, Mr. Thing," you say, standing up.

But before you can finish your sentence, the room starts to reel and fade. Finally, it dissolves.

Turn to page 61.

You trudge past the orchid-covered tree in search of the crossroads. You pass it again, some hours later. At least you *think* it's some hours later. It's dark now and you're feeling faint from hunger and exhaustion. Maybe you better lie down and try to sleep.

You are never seen or heard of again.

Did you meet a fate in the jungle similar to Jim Thompson's? No one can tell. Your disappearance adds another strange chapter to the unsolved mystery of the Thai Silk King.

The End

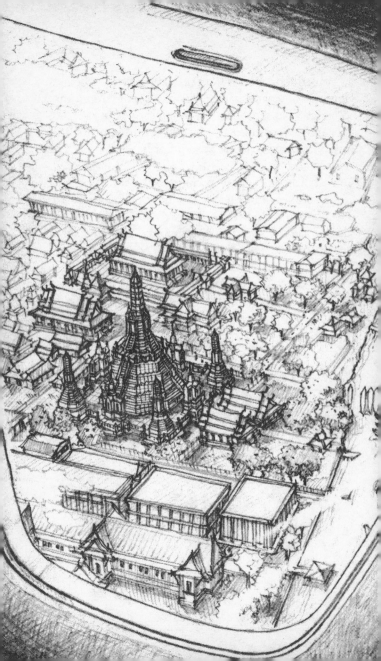

Twelve hours later, you're boarding a flight to Bangkok. You've wired ahead to your friend Ning Thanom about your trip. Ning was a Thai exchange student at your school three years ago, and the two of you became good friends. If nothing else comes of this search for Jim Thompson, at least you'll enjoy seeing Ning.

Shortly after takeoff, you fall sound asleep. You are awakened many hours later by the sound of the flight attendant's voice announcing your final approach into Bangkok. She points out the shimmering pagoda of Wat Arun, the Temple of Dawn, below. It's raining lightly, and you remember that it's still the monsoon season here, when it rains on and off every day. Your poncho should come in handy.

Turn to page 21.

Quiet steps approach you from the stairwell. Your pulse quickens. Oh, no! Someone can't have found out about your discovery yet! You whirl around to face your enemy. It's . . . the librarian.

"I'm very sorry," she whispers, "but the library is about to close for the day. If you'd like, you can come back tomorrow morning at 9 AM." You thank her, palms sweating, and leave.

Back in your office, you stare at the ceiling, wondering what could have been in the missing articles. If you can find out, you'll be on to Thompson's trail. Your thoughts are interrupted by Sam, returning with the mystery envelope. He tells you the fingerprint scan didn't turn up a thing. As soon as he leaves, the telephone rings.

You pick up the receiver. "What is it?" you say grumpily.

"Why aren't you on your way to Thailand?" a man's voice asks.

"What? Who are you?" you demand. "And what right is it of yours to know?"

"I'm the man who hired you," the voice says calmly. "I'm just curious about why you didn't take your flight tonight."

Go on to the next page.

"I'll tell you why I didn't take my flight!" you snap. "First, I barely know anything about Thompson. Second, I get the idea that if Thompson didn't vanish in the jungle, the people who kidnapped him aren't going to be that eager to have someone find him after all this time. And third, I know it's just this funny thing I've got, but I like to meet a client before going to work for him."

You surprise yourself at your strong reaction and you realize you really care about this case. You wait for the man's reaction, expecting him to hang up.

Turn to page 23.

18

"Jim Thompson was staying with friends in the Cameron Highlands for Easter when he disappeared," Mr. Sing tells you. "From all accounts, it was a perfectly pleasant, perfectly typical house party weekend."

"Who were his hosts?" you ask.

"Helen and T. G. Ling," Mr. Sing replies, "both of whom Thompson had known for years. The only other house guest, a woman, was also an old and trusted friend."

Mr. Sing continues: "On Saturday they did the usual things—a little shopping, a walk, a large lunch, a long nap, and a dinner party that night. On Sunday the four went to Easter services before leaving on a picnic. And the picnic is the first time that anyone remembers anything being odd."

"Like what?" you ask.

Turn to page 12.

The air inside the Bangkok airport is hot and steamy. By the time you clear customs, your clothes are soaking with sweat. You push through glass doors to the arrival area outside. It's chaos. People run back and forth, cars honk, children cry, and a luggage rack falls over in front of you. Pedicabs, a kind of bicycle rickshaw, battle with imposing black limousines for parking spaces and customers. You're headed for the cab stand when a familiar voice behind you says, "Welcome to Thailand!"

You whip around. "Ning!" you exclaim, hugging your friend. She gives you the warmest welcoming smile. Thailand after all is known as "The Land of Smiles."

Turn to page 22.

"So you came to Thailand to look for Jim Thompson?" Ning asks, though this time with a different kind of smile.

"Yes, but I'm afraid I don't know very much about him yet. My assignment came up suddenly and mysteriously. I had to leave before I had a chance to research the case," you answer.

"I have an offer to make that might interest you, then," Ning says. "Just by chance I'm going to the Cameron Highlands this weekend to visit friends. That's the resort in Malaysia where Thompson originally disappeared. I came out here this morning to invite you along. It might be a good place to start your research. But if you don't want to come, I can arrange a meeting for you with a mystery writer my parents know. Sen Sing has studied the Thompson case inside and out for years. He knows more about Thompson's disappearance than anybody else in Bangkok."

If you say, "I'd love to go to Malaysia,"
turn to page 28.

If you say, "I'd rather talk to Mr. Sing and
recover from my flight," turn to page 30.

But the man on the phone sounds apologetic. "You're right," he says. "I should have written a note, but I couldn't. I, well . . . it's a long story. I suppose we could meet as long as we make it look accidental."

"Where?" you demand. The person on the line does sound strange.

The man is silent for a moment. "The Lincoln Memorial in Washington, D.C., at nine tomorrow morning. We'll pretend we're tourists who start up a conversation by chance. I'll be wearing a gray suit and carrying a cane. I can't talk any longer. Goodbye."

The line goes dead.

Could this be a trap? Why is everything so secret? This client is getting to be as spooky as the case!

Maybe you should call the CIA, explain the situation, and ask for a "tail" at your meeting tomorrow morning. On the other hand, if your client really does have a reason to keep all this secret, calling in the CIA would only mess things up.

If you decide to risk going to the Lincoln Memorial alone, turn to page 27.

If you decide to call the CIA and ask for a "tail" at your meeting in the morning, turn to page 24.

24

Your instincts tell you that it would be safer to call the CIA, so you telephone the agency and briefly describe what's been going on. They immediately send over an agent named Leonard Farce. Mr. Farce grills you in detail about the contents of the envelope and your strange phone call tonight.

"That was all that came—the money, the ticket, and the news article on Thompson?"

You nod.

"Have you had everything checked for fingerprints?"

"Of course," you answer. "Sergeant Wimble had everything done for me at the police forensic lab. They didn't come up with a thing."

"What time did you receive this phone call?"

"At eight-thirty," you reply, "just about half an hour after the flight I was ticketed on left."

"How old would you say the man was from his voice?"

"Thirties, I guess," you answer thoughtfully.

"Are you sure he wasn't older than that?"

"I couldn't really tell," you reply, adding, "I'm sure he has something to do with those articles missing from the library. He would have—"

"There will be three of us there tomorrow morning," Mr. Farce suddenly says, cutting the conversation short. "Two men will be hiding nearby, and I'll be pretending to be a tourist like yourself."

You're surprised that Leonard Farce thinks three men are needed. It seems overly cautious, but you decide not to say anything.

Turn to page 44.

The next day you travel to Washington, D.C., and go to the Lincoln Memorial alone. At 9:05 AM, an old man wearing a gray suit hobbles up beside you.

"Pretty impressive, isn't he?" the old man says, pointing at the white marble statue of Lincoln.

You nod in agreement.

"I come here often," he continues in a chatty voice, "but my favorite time to come is at night."

"At night?" you ask surprised. The old man has turned around and is slowly moving away, toward the steps. Casually, you do the same.

"Yes. No one around then. The Washington Monument lit up in the distance. The whole feeling is magic," he replies.

By this time you're out of everyone's earshot, and the old man says, "Thank you for coming. I'm sure my behavior has seemed rather strange."

"Frankly, it has," you reply, helping the old man down the steps.

"Well, now that you're here, I'll be as brief and to the point as possible. My name is Sheldon Truax," he says, extending a firm hand. "I was an old friend of Jim Thompson's."

"So you were a spy, too?" you ask.

Sheldon Truax pauses, and eyes you from head to foot. "I can't tell you what I was, but it's of no importance here, anyway. Let's just say I was a person Jim Thompson felt he could trust with a dangerous secret. And in March of 1967 Thompson had a very dangerous secret."

Turn to page 34.

"Great!" Ning answers, leading you to an empty pedicab. "But before we go to Malaysia, let's get something to eat."

After a quick Thai breakfast of rice and a spicy soup made with shrimp and lemongrass, you head back to the airport for your flight to Penang, a city in northern Malaysia. In Penang, you hire a car and driver for the final leg of your journey to the town where Ning's friends live.

At a dinner in your honor that night, you're introduced to Reginald Kaye, a retired major in the British army.

"I happened to be in the Highlands that Easter weekend back in sixty-seven," he tells you, "and I was a member of the initial search party."

"Would you mind talking with me about it, Major Kaye?" you ask.

"Why, not a bit. Would love to, actually. The appearance of those photos at the Bangkok Post has got my mind thinking on it again. Can't tell you how frustrating it was back then to find not so much as a footprint. How about coming to my hotel at nine tomorrow morning?"

"That would be fine," you agree.

"Good. I'll take you up to Moonlight Cottage first off. That was the house where Thompson was staying when it all happened. From there it will be quite easy to show you the area of jungle that we covered in the search."

Go on to the next page.

That night after dinner, you fall straight to sleep. You dream that you're walking along a dirt road with jungle on both sides. The road leads uphill to a large Victorian house in a clearing. The door is open so you walk in. Inside you hear the creak creak, creak-creak of someone in a rocking chair. It's your grandmother.

She stands up. "I'm so glad you've come, child," she says. "I've been waiting for you. I have something to tell you about Jim Thompson. You are looking in the wrong place. Thompson is near the river, not the mountains."

"Near the river, Grandmother?" you ask, repeating her words.

"Yes, the river." She nods.

"But what river?"

Your grandmother smiles sadly and shakes her head. Then she walks past you out of the room.

"Grandmother, wait!" you yell. "What river? What riv—"

Suddenly you bolt upright, awakened by the sound of your own voice.

What a creepy dream! You have to tell Ning. But you hate to wake her.

If you decide not to wake Ning, turn to page 46.

If you decide to wake up Ning and tell her your dream, turn to page 116.

30

Ning goes to a phone booth and calls Sen Sing. He agrees to talk and invites you over for that afternoon at one o'clock.

"My plane to Malaysia leaves in a couple of hours," Ning tells you, "so I can't come. But I'll call you Monday as soon as I'm back. I hope Mr. Sing can help!"

You thank your friend and grab a pedicab. By the time you reach the Oriental Hotel in downtown Bangkok, you have just enough time for a shower and a change of clothes before going on to Mr. Sing's.

His house is number 13 on a quiet, tree-lined street, just a few yards from a bustling avenue. You ring the bell, and Mr. Sing himself answers.

"Ah, welcome. You must be Ning's friend," he says, extending his hand. "Please come in and sit down."

Mr. Sing ushers you into an opulent living room filled with antique Thai furniture and an impressive collection of carved wooden Buddhas. He waves you into a chair.

"Studying the Jim Thompson case has been a favorite hobby of mine for years," he begins. "What would you like to know?"

"For starters, I'd like to know more about the disappearance itself," you reply.

A servant enters with tea and cakes while Mr. Sing begins.

Turn to page 18.

Early the next day you lead six Malaysian police back out to the cave. Once again no one is there, but the fire ashes are still warm. The police set up an ambush, and you wait for many hours. Finally someone approaches, walking stealthily through the heavy jungle growth. Twenty feet away from you, the footsteps stop. His jungle years have trained him well. After a few furious sniffs, he whirls around and speeds through the forest.

Luckily, two police officers have been posted in the trees. One flings a net at the escaping figure, misses, but manages to make him trip. Four officers are on top of him in a flash. They take him back to the police station, where he is identified as the single remaining member of an Emergency terrorist group.

"You are an amazing detective," the chief of police informs you, "even if it was foolish to wander off the marked trails. You have found the leader of a horrible terrorist gang in a place we gave up searching years back. May I express the thanks of all the Malaysian people."

You are flown with Ning to Kuala Lumpur, the capital of Malaysia. The prime minister presents you with the highest award given to foreigners and grants you honorary Malaysian citizenship.

Somehow, your search for Jim Thompson gets lost in the shuffle. Your trip turned out to be a success after all, though not in the way you would have predicted.

The End

"What kind of secret?" you ask.

Sheldon Truax sighs deeply. "That's part of the problem, I'm afraid. I've never exactly known. Jim called me a few days before he disappeared and said he had to meet me the following week. He said he needed my advice and possibly my help. Apparently Jim had stumbled upon a smuggling operation going on inside his business. He never said what was being smuggled, but from the sound of it, I guessed it was either heroin or rubies. Jim said that he needed a little more information before he could figure out who was behind the operation, but what he knew so far was enough to scare him. His exact words were, 'You're not going to believe who's involved in all of this, Sheldon.'"

"Had the smugglers realized that Thompson knew?" you ask.

"Jim didn't think so. But he was following his schedule, anyway, so no one would get suspicious. He'd made plans some time earlier to spend Easter in Malaysia and to continue on to Singapore on business the following week. We had an appointment to get together as soon as he got back to Thailand."

"And he never did," you finish.

"Correct," Truax replies.

Go on to the next page.

"Do you have any idea why Jim Thompson called you? Why didn't he just call the police or the CIA?"

"Well, as I told you, I was an old friend, in Bangkok on business for a few weeks. At first it seemed perfectly natural that he should call on me for help. It was only later that I thought it was odd, and by then I'd begun to suspect something else."

Turn to page 42.

You follow the well-worn footpath of the unmarked trail for a short way, just to see where it leads. The bushes and plants, which have not been cut back, crowd in on the trail. Soon the leaves and branches get thicker and heavier. Your face and hands are covered with scratches, and you're dripping wet. Finally the trail underfoot comes to a dead end.

You're about to turn around when you smell a faint whiff of smoke. You sniff some more and follow the scent. Suddenly you stumble out of the heavy brush into a small clearing. In front of you is a cooking fire, and the ashes are still warm!

You read in the paper that Thompson had been trained in jungle survival by the Army OSS. Could he possibly have made a life for himself here? You eye the clearing carefully. At one end, the vines and hanging moss seem irregular and bunched up. You walk closer, then stop. You're at the opening to a cave!

You want to explore the inside, but what happens if someone comes back while you're there? You'd have no way to escape and no way to defend yourself. Maybe it would be smarter to find a good hiding place and wait to see who returns.

If you enter the cave to take a look, turn to page 50.

If you hide someplace where you can see if anyone returns to the cave, turn to page 90.

When you get back to your office, the plane ticket to Bangkok is missing. Leonard Farce is going to have some explaining to do, you think. But that afternoon the phone is silent. Farce doesn't call you until the next day.

"I'm sorry," he tells you, "but this case is of utmost importance to our national security. We're going to have to take it away from you. Your plane ticket has been cashed in. You should receive a refund next week."

"But what about the old man? Who is he? Where did you take him?" you cry.

"What old man?" Leonard Farce asks you in a perfectly innocent voice.

The End

After reading the small white slip of paper, you bow to the statue, thanking the Buddha. If the weight on your shoulders is your search for Thompson, it seems you're going to find him soon! You smile. The old man from the *ja* stick booth suddenly appears at your side. "Good fortune, I hope. Ready to go see the head monk?"

You nod and follow him to the doorway. Just as you step outside, a chunk of mortar from the wall being repaired comes loose. It hurtles downward, missing the man next to you by inches but hitting you in the skull and killing you instantly.

Was it an accident? Or was the chunk of mortar deliberately dropped? During the police investigation all the witnesses say they could not tell. One thing is certain: your fortune came true and much sooner than you expected.

The End

You pull out one of the smoke bombs and set it on the jungle floor. As soon as you light it, the bomb jumps and twists, darting right off the trail into some heavy undergrowth. You crawl on your hands and knees after it. But where did it go?

Whoa! Suddenly you're staring over the edge of a steep, twenty-foot drop. The smoke bomb is there, all right, lying right next to a human skeleton, partly covered with moss and vines.

Turn to page 51.

42

"Like what?" you ask.

"Like maybe the CIA itself was somehow involved in the smuggling," Truax replies. "I got in touch with them as soon as the story about Jim broke. But they treated my information in an incredibly casual fashion." Truax pauses before adding, "I wasn't the only one who suspected the CIA, either. Several people complained about their sloppy attitude toward the entire investigation. But, of course, I was the only one who knew about the smuggling."

"What did you do next?" you ask.

"I investigated on my own for three whole months. I made some enemies in the process. But I didn't come up with a thing," Truax tells you. "Jim's fate has bothered me ever since."

"Why were you so secretive about hiring me?" you finally ask.

"Well, I thought you might not accept the assignment if you knew how potentially dangerous it was," Truax responds.

"I have to admit, it sounds a lot more dangerous than it did at first," you agree. "Especially since I'll be working alone."

Go on to the next page.

Sheldon Truax thinks for a moment. "Well, I could go with you, I suppose. I can't do any of the field work, of course," he says, pointing to his leg. "Bum knee. But I could keep a secret headquarters at the Oriental Hotel and give you what knowledge of the country I have. That might help."

If you decide to accept Sheldon Truax's offer to come with you to Thailand, turn to page 54.

If you decide to decline Truax's offer and go to Thailand alone, turn to page 57.

44

Early the next morning you arrive in Washington, D.C. By 8:30, you're at the Lincoln Memorial. For a full half hour, you have to try to look like a tourist. Leonard Farce stands casually off in a corner, looking as if he's been a tourist all his life.

Finally, a few minutes before nine, a man dressed in a gray suit approaches the monument. His hair is pure white, and he hobbles slowly with the use of a cane. You suddenly get the funny feeling that calling in the CIA was a big mistake.

The old man is heading in your direction, but he hasn't seen Leonard Farce yet. When he does, the effect is immediate. He stops short, throws you an angry glance, and whirls around to leave.

What happens next is almost unreal. Leonard Farce rushes past you after the old man. Five—not two—hidden agents appear out of nowhere and follow. Together the six men overpower the man who is putting up quite a fight.

"Why did you betray me?" the old man bellows in your direction. The sound of his accusing voice echoes eerily inside the marble chamber.

The six CIA agents handcuff the old man and rush him down the monument's steps into a waiting black sedan.

"Wait!" you scream at Farce. "Wait! What's going on?"

"We'll call you later!" Farce yells out the window before driving off.

Turn to page 38.

46

You can tell Ning about the dream in the morning.

In a few minutes you're fast asleep. The next thing you know it's light out and your clock says 8:35. You're supposed to meet Major Kaye in twenty-five minutes!

You skip breakfast and rush to the hotel. Major Kaye is waiting for you on the porch. Shaking your hand, he says, "Hop in my car. Even though the cottage is close by, it'll be easier. I've called the caretaker and he says it's fine to go up for a look."

The road leading to Moonlight Cottage is steep, narrow, and twisting. Dense jungle surrounds the cottage on all sides. The monsoon rains, more like a mist, fall gently.

"It's awfully isolated, isn't it?" you ask.

"Yes. There's a rumor that this cottage was once a headquarters for a group of rebels during the Malaysian Emergency," he answers.

"What was the Emergency?"

"It's what we called the period from 1948 to 1960, when bands of Communist terrorists hid out in the countryside. Many of them were near here. They would ambush Malaysian soldiers and police—sometimes even tourists—capture them, and kill them. Many executions are supposed to have taken place in the rose garden out back."

Go on to the next page.

"What happened in 1960?" you ask.

"The government finally got the upper hand and declared the Emergency officially over. Most of the terrorists took to the jungle. Some people say they're still out there," Major Kaye adds cheerfully.

Turn to page 52.

The map instructions said you might have to wait where you are for twenty-four hours. You look around. Just ahead, at the edge of the trail, you spot a fallen log. You sit down, make yourself comfortable, and wait. An hour passes, then another. You look at your watch. Two o'clock. By now someone—Ning or Major Kaye—must at least realize you're missing. If no one has found you by dusk, you decide, you'll light up one of the smoke bombs.

You're half-dozing when the sharp snap of a twig jerks you full awake. They've found you!

You look up eagerly and see a Bengal tiger, a rare, but real, danger to any trekker through the jungles of Southeast Asia.

Little did you know that her lair with three unguarded cubs lies ten feet off in the jungle, and she sees you as a threat. She lunges at you, and the weight of her pounce kills you instantly. Hurrying off to check on her babies, the tigress leaves your body to be discovered by rescuers or some other jungle predator—whoever gets there first.

The End

50

You walk around the edge of the clearing so you won't leave any footprints. Lifting back some overhanging moss, you peer inside the cave. It's quite dim, but you can make out a crude table made from logs, a few stools, and some woven mats resting on homemade grass mattresses.

You crawl through the opening. A large mound in the rear of the cave is covered by a dirty oilcloth tarp. Gingerly lifting up one edge, you try to make out what's underneath. You reach down and touch cool, smooth metal.

"Machine guns!" you gasp.

Turn to page 76.

Could this be Thompson's skeleton? You're so excited that you forget that you're lost and begin running back down the trail to find help.

Someone has seen your smoke signal after all. A little way beyond where you set it off, you run into a birdwatching couple headed in your direction.

"Come quickly. Please," you gasp. "I've just found a skeleton in a ravine back there. I think it might be Jim Thompson!"

They hurry after you. Luckily, the man has a small climbing rope in his pack. Together the three of you are able to lift the skeleton out. You become positive that it's Thompson's when you find a gold wristwatch engraved with the initials J. T. on one of the skeleton's arms!

Turn to page 56.

Major Kaye shows you around the rest of the property, explaining how the search for Jim Thompson proceeded.

"For a week, over four hundred police and volunteers combed the jungle surrounding the cottage. After the fifth day, we suspected the chance that Thompson would come out alive was slim," Major Kaye tells you. "But what demoralized everyone was that by week's end we hadn't even a clue. Not a footprint or broken twig or shred of clothing. By then people had begun to think he'd been kidnapped."

"What do you think happened to Jim Thompson?" you ask.

"In my opinion?" Major Kaye says, staring out into the thick jungle growth. "Well, one of the search-party leaders once said it would take an entire regiment of trained personnel a month to cover the surrounding jungle properly. And who's to say Thompson didn't walk even beyond that area? In my opinion, Thompson is still out there."

"The Highlands are supposed to be a popular spot for walking. Are there any trails near here?" you inquire.

"Plenty. One starts right over there." Major Kaye points at a slight indentation in the bushes. "I was just about to show you."

Turn to page 58.

Having accepted Sheldon Truax's offer to accompany you to Bangkok, you suqqest he make new travel arrangements as quickly as possible. Two days later you're in the lobby of the Oriental Hotel, checking into your rooms. The flight was a long one, and you're exhausted. You agree to meet for dinner after you've both had a good nap.

You wake up in late afternoon and step outside on the terrace. Even though it's still the monsoon season, the clouds have parted temporarily, and the sun is shining. You gaze at the busy river full of boats. There are school children in ferries, merchants paddling narrow fruit-laden canoes, and wide-bellied slow-moving houseboats. On the opposite shore a gorgeous pagoda, the mark of a Buddhist temple, shimmers in the sun as if it were covered in sequins. Some of the smaller boats head into klongs—canals— on that side of the river. Earlier you read in the guidebook that Bangkok is criss-crossed with a network

of these narrow canals. You are about to step back inside your room when activity on a small wharf right next to the hotel catches your eye.

You watch as two wiry men dressed in shorts load a squirming sack onto their green boat. You're wondering what kind of animal is inside when suddenly its head pops out.

It's Sheldon Truax!

Turn to page 62.

56

Your appearance back in town causes quite a stir. It seems as if everyone for miles around comes to the police station to gaze at the skeleton and get the autograph of its amazing finder. Meanwhile the chief of the local police places a call to the Thai Silk Company in Bangkok.

"I know this sounds odd," he begins, "but a tourist here, wandering around off a remote walking trail, has just discovered a skeleton wearing a watch with the initials J. T. . . . Yes, the watch was gold . . . You mean it could be Jim Thompson?! . . . Yes, yes, the tourist is right here . . . Yes, I'm sure that's all right."

The chief hangs up the phone and turns to you. "The Thai Silk Company is sending a private plane to pick you up immediately and take you back to Bangkok. They are incredibly excited."

Turn to page 64.

"I think it's better if I go to Thailand alone," you tell Sheldon Truax. "If the CIA knows I'm working for you, things could get sticky. Besides, I have a good friend who lives in Bangkok. I'm sure she can help."

"That's fine with me," Sheldon Truax replies. "Here's my card. Call me as soon as you learn anything."

"I will," you promise, shaking the old man's hand goodbye.

Back at home you stuff your backpack with a sleeping bag, rain gear, two pairs of sneakers, and light, loose clothing for the tropics. Before you know it, you are sitting high over the Pacific Ocean in a jumbo jet bound for Bangkok. Staring up at the ceiling, you go over all the elements of the case. Today's newspapers reported that, now, some of Thompson's searchers seem to be missing. Whoever was involved in Thompson's kidnap—CIA or not—obviously isn't excited at the prospect of seeing him returned alive.

You'll have to be on the lookout for booby traps or false information. But at least you've got one advantage:

"Nobody ever suspects a kid," you think, chuckling to yourself.

Turn to page 66.

58

There is a web of well-marked trails in the jungle all around the cottage. Major Kaye gives you a brisk tour of several of them. After you walk one trail for forty-five minutes, it ends in a T. The Major pulls out a map of all the trails and points to your location.

"This is as far as the detailed search for Thompson went. People searched beyond here, of course, but it was more informal."

Major Kaye glances at his watch. "I'd show you more, but I've got to go," he says. "Why don't you stay here and keep looking around? You can have the map. I'll find my way out alone. Stick to the marked trails and you won't have any problems. If you get lost, there are instructions on the map's lower left corner."

You thank Major Kaye for all his help and watch him walk back down the trail. Suddenly he turns around and runs back.

"Wait!" he shouts, "I almost forgot." He reaches into his shirt pocket. "Take these smoke bombs," he says. "If you do get seriously lost, you can use them to signal your location. Good luck now, and cheerio."

Go on to the next page.

In a few seconds, he has disappeared from view.

You turn to your right, being careful to follow your route on the map. No one else seems to be out hiking. You're not surprised, considering how wet it is.

A half hour later, you come to a partly hidden trail branching off to the left. You look at the map, but the trail isn't marked. Yet the pathway visible through the uncut brush looks well worn.

You remember Major Kaye's words: "Stick to the marked trails . . . " But can it really hurt to venture a few yards off?

If you decide to explore the unmarked trail, turn to page 36.

If you decide to stick to the trail you're on, turn to page 8.

You wake up in a small, dimly lit room. You're lying on a bed. Your hands and feet are tied, and you've been gagged. Mr. Sing sits on another bed watching you.

"So you think you can find Jim Thompson, do you?" he asks sarcastically. "I've been researching the Thompson case for nineteen years! I'm not going to let some lousy kid find him before I do."

You try to talk, but nothing comes out.

Mr. Sing stands to leave. "Behave and you won't be hurt. Any tricks and you're a dead duck," he snarls.

Over the next few days Mr. Sing keeps you well fed. He also gives you injections that make you drowsy all day. You are awake just long enough to figure out that Sing's house is currently the head-quarters for a huge search effort. People come and go at all hours of the night. The phone rings nonstop, and you frequently hear the sound of Thompson's name.

Turn to page 65.

You dash out of your room and through the lobby of the hotel. You arrive at the wharf just as the boat carrying Sheldon Truax enters a canal on the other side of the river and disappears. Frantically waving, you manage to catch the attention of a passing water taxi, those Thai craft known as long tail boats which use car engines for power.

"Head toward that canal opposite!" you tell the driver, jumping in. "I'm chasing two men in a narrow green boat."

The boatman expertly maneuvers his craft through the swollen currents and speeds into the canal. You hold on for dear life as the hull slaps against the wake of other boats. A quarter-mile later you spot the green boat tied to a dock on your right.

"Stop here!" you order.

"But the snake farm is closed," your driver protests.

You look up at the sign on a metal-link fence for the first time. It says THONBURI SNAKE FARM. DANGEROUS ANIMALS WITHIN! NO TRESPASSING! But that's got to be the right boat, you think, checking the green craft again. Just then you notice that the gate looks slightly open. You could go in after the two men. But maybe you should go find a canal police officer to enter with you.

If you walk into the snake farm to rescue Sheldon Truax alone, turn to page 78.

If you look for a canal police officer to accompany you inside, turn to page 69.

The next day Ning explains to your hostess why you're leaving. Your hostess accepts the explanation without surprise. In fact, she encourages you to go. A few hours later, you find yourself back on the winding five-hour journey to Penang.

As you and Ning try to decide what rivers to look near first, your hired car suddenly stops in the middle of nowhere. A man runs out of the bushes and changes places with the driver, who slides over on the front seat next to him. Ning watches all this without comment, but she probably missed the article you saw in that morning's paper about the recent return of the dreaded Malaysian kidnap gangs.

Without another thought, you fling your door open and leap from the speeding car. The last thing you remember is Ning standing over you in a ditch saying, "What did you do that for? Are you out of your mind?"

Turn to page 77.

64

Late that day, you fly back to Bangkok. Jim Thompson's skeleton lies safely packed in a wooden box next to you, and his watch is in your pocket. When you arrive in Bangkok there's a crowd waiting to greet you. The mayor hands you a key to the city, and you're sped by police motorcade to an audience at the king's palace. By the next morning, your story is front-page news around the world.

Turn to page 105.

One night, the commotion is so great that you are awakened from your drugged stupor.

"He's in Ayutthaya!" You hear someone shout before your world becomes silent once again.

On the fourth day, the servant who brings you your dinner shakes you awake. But instead of feeding you, he begins to untie your ropes.

A spasm of fear grips your stomach. Maybe Sing has decided to do away with you after all!

If you try to make a run for it as soon as your feet are untied, turn to page 99.

If you decide to wait for a better chance to escape, turn to page 70.

The Oriental Hotel in Bangkok is large and luxurious, right on the banks of the Chao Phraya River. The first thing you do when you get there is call your good friend Ning Thanom. But she isn't in. Her mother tells you that Ning's gone to Malaysia and won't be back for a week.

You go out onto your balcony and watch the action on the river absent-mindedly. Your original plan was to go with Ning to Sisaket, the town that the photos of Thompson were sent from, and ask about him at all the nearby temples. Now you'll have to go alone. Without Ning's extra eyes and ears, it's especially important for you to be wide awake tomorrow. You go back inside your room and order a dinner of marinated beef shish kebab

with a spicy peanut sauce from room service. Then you go straight to bed.

The next morning the Bangkok Post arrives with breakfast. Two more people who were searching for Thompson have disappeared, bringing the total missing to five. Sisaket seems like a dangerous place to be these days. You wish you knew of some other place to start looking!

Just then you glance down, and another article catches your eye.

Turn to page 68.

MONKS TO MEET IN NORTH

A large convention of Buddhist monks will be taking place this week in the city of Udon Thani. Papers will be given on several aspects of modern-day Hinayana Buddhism. Two Zen monks from Daitokuji Temple in Kyoto, Japan will also attend. They plan to talk on the relationship between Zen meditation and meditation practiced by Thai monks.

Two thousand monks from all over the country are expected to be there.

After you finish reading the article, a thought flashes through your mind. Maybe Jim Thompson will be there, or at least some monks who know him. Perhaps you should go to Udon Thani.

If you decide to leave for Sisaket as you planned, turn to page 73.

If you try to find Thompson at the monks' convention instead, turn to page 74.

"We have to find the police," you tell your driver.

He gives you a funny look but backs the boat away from the dock without saying anything. A short while later, you round the corner of a narrow klong. There's a police officer in a boat just ahead.

"Officer! Officer! I need your help. My friend was kidnapped by two men, and I think they've taken him to the snake farm. I'm afraid they might try to kill him!" you exclaim. "I want you to enter the snake farm with me."

The officer hasn't been looking at you while you talked. He seems more interested in your boat. Finally he says, "I'm placing you under arrest."

"WHAT? Arrest? Arrest me for what?" you ask in disbelief.

"For stealing this boat," the officer tells you.

"But . . . but . . . I didn't steal this boat! I rented it from him," you say, turning to point to your driver. But your driver has disappeared!

"Well, kid, you'll have to explain that at headquarters," the police officer tells you.

The End

70

When the servant has finished untying your ropes, he motions you to be silent and to climb on his back. He carries you down the back steps and out to a klong—one of the narrow waterways that crisscross Bangkok—at the rear of Sing's house. Ning is waiting in a long tail motorboat at the water's edge.

"Ning!" you whisper. "What are you doing here?"

"No time to talk now. Let's get going," she replies.

Turn to page 80.

You steer the boat straight into the marsh and kill the engine. The reeds tear at your face and your rain-soaked clothing, but the swampy marsh proves an ideal hiding spot. A few seconds later Sing's boat speeds by. He doesn't even glance in your direction.

"How did you figure out I'd been kidnapped?" you ask Ning as soon as Sen Sing's boat disappears.

"I called the hotel. They said you'd checked in but never returned," Ning replies, "so I knew something had happened to you Friday afternoon. Mr. Sing swore he had no idea where you were. But I bribed one of the servants. He told me the truth and agreed to help rescue you."

"Sing is crazy! He has a huge search for Thompson underway," you tell Ning. "The reason he kidnapped me was to prevent me finding Thompson first."

"Did you learn anything that might help us find Thompson?" she asks.

"Well, I did hear someone say he's in Ayutthaya," you reply.

"Ayutthaya!" Ning exclaims. "That's right up the river from Bangkok. We can get there by boat tonight."

"Tonight?" you ask in wonder. "What about your arm?"

"My arm is fine," Ning responds. "I was planning to camp in the boat, anyway. We can't go back to my house or the hotel. Sing will be looking for us there."

"Okay," you agree. "Let's untangle the weeds from the propeller and get going."

Turn to page 91.

The next morning you travel to Sisaket by train. Unfortunately, most of the countryside you pass through is shrouded in a monsoon mist. You can't tell what it's like. Occasionally, you glimpse some rice paddies or jungle-covered hills in the distance. But when you arrive in Sisaket a few hours later, you haven't learned much about what kinds of terrain to expect in your search for Thompson.

At the station you get directions to the main temple. There you plan to talk to the head monk about Thompson. First, though, you stop for some lunch: a fiery hot curry followed by some chewy coconut sweets and soda.

Turn to page 81.

74

You head for Udon Thani to look for Jim Thompson at the monks' conference. The town is in the north, a long train ride from Bangkok, and it pours rain the whole way. You overhear on someone's radio that the monsoon rains have been especially heavy this year.

When you arrive, you are greeted by the sight of thousands of monks milling about the town. They all sport shaved heads, orange robes, and umbrellas. They only differ in size and age. Some monks are fat, some are skinny; some look no older than five, others look to be in their eighties. Somewhere, in the middle of all this, you hope to spot Jim Thompson.

Turn to page 82.

You turn and run wildly out of the cave toward the unmarked trail. Leaves and branches tear at your face and rip your clothing, but you hardly notice. Finally you reach the footpath. You feel a huge surge of relief but you keep running all the way into town and straight to the police station.

Bursting through the front door, you shout, "I found a hideout in the jungle!"

Two police officers sit at their desks on duty. The one leaning back in his chair falls over backwards. The other one stands up. "You found what?" he says.

"A hideout in the jungle near an unmarked trail. There's a cave filled with machine guns there!" you exclaim breathlessly.

Turn to page 33.

You wake up in a missionary hospital. You've broken your right hip, and you're in traction. Ning stands at the foot of the bed. The two men from the hired car stand next to her looking worried.

"What, may I ask," says Ning, seeing you awake, "were you trying to prove by jumping out of the car?"

"I thought we were being kidnapped. I just read in the paper this morning about a lot of recent kidnappings," you say sheepishly.

Ning translates this to the two men. One of them answers her, and the three of them laugh till the tears run down their faces.

"Well?" you say after a little while, feeling left out.

"The first driver just didn't have his license in that province," Ning says, still laughing. "He arranged to pick up his friend who did."

You try to laugh, too, but it hurts. Besides, your search for Jim Thompson is over, and you don't find that too funny.

Your hip finally heals, but you walk with a slight limp for the rest of your life. Fifty years later, when your grandchildren ask about your limp, you sit them all around you in a circle and begin to tell them the tale of the mysterious disappearance of Jim Thompson. And as the years go by, your story about how you got the limp in the search for the Silk King gets more and more heroic.

The End

The gate to the snake farm swings back with a whine. You step past an empty ticket booth and inside the walled compound. Slowly you size up the situation. The snake farm turns out to be filled with a lot more than snakes. It appears to be some kind of zoo.

You advance slowly past the monkey cages. A sulking panther growls at you from behind bars.

"Hey, pal, I'm not in such a great mood myself," you whisper.

At the other end of a row of cages you spot a small building. The door is open and the lights are on. Maybe they brought Mr. Truax inside?

Go on to the next page.

You move as quietly as possible toward the building. On the way your attention is taken by three huge and deadly king cobras twisted together in the bottom of a deep pit.

You bend further over the rails to check that Sheldon Truax wasn't disposed of there. Suddenly two strong arms grasp you from behind and push you forward. You flip over the railing and tumble eight feet below.

"Help!" you scream. "Help me!"

But your attacker has disappeared, gone to let your boat-taxi go. Desperately you try scaling the damp and slimy walls, but it's no use.

In the meantime, one of the king cobras untangles itself from its friends and makes its way slowly toward you.

The End

80

As soon as you're in the boat, the servant gives it a stiff push and darts into the bushes. Ning starts to paddle. You're one hundred feet away when huge floodlights come on at the house.

Sing has found out you're gone!

He runs down to his boathouse followed by two thugs. They jump into a boat like yours, and a motor zings to life. Ning drops the paddles and starts up the engine. The chase is on!

Ning has a good lead, but Mr. Sing's boat is gaining. As it gets closer, he begins to shoot. "My arm!" Ning gasps in pain. She's been hit! You grab the steering wheel.

"Are you okay?" you shout above the din. Ning nods. She's making a tourniquet out of an old rag in the bottom of the boat.

Just then another shot whizzes by, only inches from your ear. You open up to full throttle and your boat bursts forward.

You turn a sharp corner. It's hard to see in the dark, but there seems to be a marsh straight ahead. You might just have time to disappear inside it and kill the engine before Sing comes around the corner after you.

If you try to hide in the marsh, turn to page 71.

If you continue on the klong past the marsh, turn to page 86.

After lunch you find the temple easily. You walk inside its cool, shaded courtyard lined with statues of the Buddha. Monks and visitors walk back and forth. Some workers on an elaborate bamboo scaffolding are repairing the walls of the main hall.

Just inside its entrance, the *ja* stick booth—a Thai fortunetelling stand—is doing a brisk business.

Seeing you, a tiny old man walks up and says, "Come shake the *ja* sticks. Have your fortune told, your future predicted! You need your fortune, I can tell!"

"I'm sorry, but I don't need my fortune told," you reply. You hope he'll stop bothering you.

"Then why are you here?" the man persists.

"I'm looking for the head monk. I need to talk to him," you say in exasperation.

"I know where he is," the man tells you. "I can take you to him myself. But surely you have time to shake the *ja* sticks first?" He smiles.

If you say "yes," turn to page 89.

If you say, "Please take me to the head monk. I'll come back for my fortune later," turn to page 94.

After checking into a hotel, you make your way to the convention registration booth inside a local temple. There you ask a sweet-faced, patient monk if anyone named Jim Thompson has registered for the conference.

"No," he replies after checking some papers. "No one by that name."

Your heart sinks. Then you ask, "Are any foreign monks scheduled to attend?"

The monk checks his lists again and answers, "Yes, there are two foreigners from central Thailand scheduled to arrive late today."

"Can I leave a message for them?" you ask.

"Of course," the monk replies politely.

You don't know if they'll pay attention to your note, but it's worth a try. You scribble down your name and the address of your hotel. You're afraid to tell them the real reason you want to meet, so you add that you're thinking of joining a Buddhist monastery and need to ask some questions.

Go on to the next page.

Slowly you return to your hotel to wait. It's still raining very hard, and from the look of the sullen gray clouds overhead, it's not about to stop.

You throw yourself down on the bed and hear a small crackle from under your pillow. Cautiously, you lift the pillow. Beneath it is a small, folded paper with your name written in large letters on top. You open it and read:

I can tell you about Jim Thompson.
Meet me at Deng's Restaurant at 430.

You glance at your watch. It's four o'clock. You hurry down and ask at the desk for directions to Deng's Restaurant.

"It's on Napralarn Road on the outskirts of town," the clerk tells you, "but I wouldn't go there today if I were you. That's in the low-lying part of town, and they've just issued a flood alert. That area will be inundated."

You thank the clerk and go to the front door, where you pause and try to decide what to do. Should you follow the clerk's advice and stay here? Or should you risk the flooding? Meeting whoever wrote you the note might be your only chance to discover anything.

On the other hand, you could be walking into a trap.

If you go to Deng's Restaurant, turn to page 85.

If you stay at the hotel, hoping your informant will contact you again, turn to page 96.

You approach a cab idling quietly at the hotel's steps.

"Take me to Deng's Restaurant on Napralarn Road," you say.

"Floods out that way, you know," the driver answers. "But it's okay if we hurry. Hop in!"

The driver speeds along the monk-filled streets, and you begin to relax. There's no sign of flooding as far as you can tell.

Suddenly the next street you turn into is covered by a few inches of water. "Look out!" you exclaim.

Your driver turns around. "Don't worry," he says. "Flood's not bad. Same every year."

You nod uneasily and gaze at the muddy water. Your cab comes to a stop at a light. As you wait, the water level rises several inches. In another minute it has reached the level of the taxi's electrical system. It shorts out, and the engine goes dead.

"Don't worry, don't worry," your driver says, as he climbs out and opens the hood. You get out to see if you can help, but it's too late. A current of water hurtles up the street, sweeping away you, your driver, and the cab.

Along with thousands of others in Udon Thani, you become a casualty of the worst floods in the history of the region.

The End

"We're not far from the river," Ning yells over the roar of the motor as you speed past the marsh. "We'll lose them there."

The klong twists past several large, elegant houses, some modern and some traditional Thai. You glimpse a huge trellis of orchids in one yard. The large creamy blossoms seem to glow in the night. Next you notice the paved courtyard of a Buddhist temple with steps right down to the water. Thailand seems even more exotic during the night than it did during the day, but you push those thoughts from your mind. Sing is in hot pursuit and up ahead you spot the Chao Phraya River, your escape route.

As you zoom out into the open water, you turn your head to see if Sing is close behind. Ning screams, but it's too late. You smack right into a sampan, one of the huge-bellied houseboats used to bring rice down from the north. You and Ning are thrown into the air, and your boat is smashed to pieces. You try swimming to shore, but the river is swollen from the monsoon rains, and the currents are treacherous. No one can see you in the dark.

Finally you give up in exhaustion, letting the river carry you out to sea and to certain death.

The End

"Oh, all right. I guess I have time," you say grudgingly. Inside the dark temple, it takes a few minutes for your eyes to become accustomed to the light. The sharp pungent smell of incense fills your nostrils. Gradually you make out the shape of an enormous old wooden Buddha. Several people kneel in front of it, praying and meditating. Some even lie flat on the floor in worship.

A young monk walks up and hands you a tall bamboo cup. Inside are the *ja* sticks, narrow strips of bamboo marked with numbers.

"Shake the cup, and choose three sticks," he instructs.

Mimicking the others near you, you kneel before the Buddha and do as the monk has said. You concentrate on your search for Thompson and your desire to find him for Sheldon Truax, reward or no reward. You stop shaking and choose three sticks that lie on top. A monk seated on a cushion consults the sticks' numbers. Then he chooses a fortune from among hundreds lying in a chest of tiny compartments before him. He hands you a small slip of paper. It says:

RIGHT NOW YOU HAVE A HEAVY
WEIGHT ON YOUR SHOULDERS.
SOON IT WILL BE LIFTED.

Turn to page 39.

90

You burrow underneath a pile of rotting ferns, leaving an opening two inches wide to watch the cave. Suddenly you hear footsteps, quiet at first, then louder, coming closer. You cower down, hoping not to be noticed. The steps stride through the underbrush. They're getting nearer. Suddenly they stop. The next minute you're being yanked from your hiding place by the hair.

An incredibly filthy man dressed in army fatigues gives you a quick, searching glance. Then he shoots you.

You have just become the most recent victim of the Malaysian Emergency.

The End

You navigate the boat out of the marsh and onto the open river. But the Chao Phraya is swollen from the monsoon rains, and the currents are tricky. Your progress upstream toward Ayutthaya is slow. Just when you think your arm will fall off from steering, Ning directs you over to a small dock at the river's edge.

"This dock belongs to a bird sanctuary," Ning tells you. "Sometimes a boatload of tourists comes out to take a look. It will be safe to sleep here for the night."

While Ning rebinds her wound, you check out the supplies she brought. You rig up a tarp to keep out the rain and lay sleeping mats on the floor of the boat. You're settling in to sleep when a flash of light in the forest grabs your attention. You watch carefully. The light flashes again.

"Ning, did you see that light?"

"What light?" she asks, turning around.

"A flashing light. In the jungle back there." You point toward the bird sanctuary.

"Oh, it's probably just fireflies. Let's go to sleep," she says drowsily.

If you go to look for the source of the light, turn to page 103.

If you follow Ning's example and try to go to sleep, turn to page 101.

92

You and Ki both sleep at the inn. The next morning Ki shakes you awake.

"Come on. It's time to go," he announces imperiously.

"But it's still dark out," you reply, sleepily rubbing your eyes.

"It's time to go," Ki repeats.

What did I get myself into? you think as you scramble to get your things.

Ki leads you out of town and straight into the jungle. All day you trudge on ancient, almost invisible, paths from temple to temple, stopping at each to ask about Jim Thompson. No one has ever heard of him.

"But Thompson could have been here and left," an old monk tells you. "In recent years many monks have fled because of guerrilla attacks by the Khmer Rouge of Cambodia." Pointing to the hills in the distance, he adds, "The guerrillas come down from those hills to capture Cambodians in refugee camps near here. Along the way, they rob and murder anyone they see."

"Rob and murder?" you gulp.

"Don't worry," Ki says tersely. "Guerrillas don't attack during the monsoon rains. For now the jungles are safe."

Turn to page 97.

"I have been waiting for you to come. I know you had difficulty getting here. Now that you are before me, listen carefully. I shall only tell my story once," he begins.

"On Easter Sunday in 1967, I had arranged to meet in secret a man well-known to me in Bangkok. He had certain information I needed. For a price he agreed to give it. The information had to do with a heroin smuggling operation I'd discovered inside my business. Unfortunately, my friend decided to sell the information elsewhere for a higher price. By the time I met him that day in the Highlands, he had gone to work for the smugglers themselves. His orders were to kill me but to make it look like an accident. I was drugged, beaten, and flown to a remote jungle near the Thai-Cambodian border, where no one could possibly think of looking for me. My kidnapper was unable to kill an old friend in cold blood. Instead he weakened me by withholding food for three days. Then he just dropped me in the jungle to die."

"What happened?" you ask, amazed.

"Something no one had counted on," Thompson tells you. "I was discovered later that day by a passing monk."

Turn to page 100.

When you promise you'll have your fortune read later, the odd little man finally agrees to take you to the head monk. He scurries into an adjoining courtyard and bows low outside a darkened doorway before entering. You do the same and are greeted by a very old monk—the abbot—seated on some rush mats with three younger monks beside him. You bow again before asking the abbot if he knows anything at all about the monk in the newspaper clipping. Unfortunately,

neither the wise-looking abbot nor his assistants have ever seen or heard of such a man.

"Could he be in a remote temple in the countryside near here?" you inquire.

"Of course," the old monk replies. "But there are many, many temples in our region. You would need a good guide to find them all!"

He strokes his chin for a few moments and says, "I have a young nephew about your age. He knows the surrounding jungles and hills very well.

He is still a bit headstrong, but I can think of no better person to lead you on your search."

"Would he work for me?" you ask.

"Come back here at five o'clock this afternoon. My nephew Ki will be waiting for you," the monk answers.

Turn to page 98.

You decide it's safer to stay at the hotel. Whoever wrote you the note will probably contact you again. Besides, those two foreign monks might show up while you're away.

A half hour later you're glad you decided to stay. Suddenly water covers the street outside the hotel. The water rises quickly, and before long it has started in through the hotel's front door.

People outside run frantically back and forth. A small child, knocked over by the rushing water, is barely saved by her screaming mother. A fat businessman staying at the hotel careens down the stairs and pushes and shoves his way through the lobby before disappearing out the door. In the meantime, rain continues to pour down as heavily as ever.

Finally, a police officer arrives. "This area is being evacuated," he announces. "All people here should leave immediately."

"But where can we go? What should we do?" someone in the lobby pleads pitifully.

"Boats are leaving from the train depot to carry people to higher ground across the flood plain," the police officer answers. "Higher ground can still be reached by foot, however, for all those strong enough. It's risky, but if you leave now, you should be all right."

If you go to the train station and try to take a boat to higher ground, turn to page 109.

If you try to get across the flood plain on foot, turn to page 104.

The guerrillas have a point there, you think, not attacking during the monsoon. You have never been so hot, wet, and uncomfortable in your life. Rain falls, off and on, all day. When the rain stops, the air becomes unbearably humid and close. By the time you find an inn that night in a town called Kantaralak, you are exhausted and irritable. To make things worse, Ki is even more silent and morose than he was before. He falls asleep grumbling.

When you wake up the next day, you get a shock. Ki isn't there! He's gone!

You run downstairs. "Have you seen my companion?" you cry.

"The boy who was with you last night?" the innkeeper asks. "He left early this morning."

"Did he say where he was going or when he's coming back?" you ask.

"No," the innkeeper replies. "He said nothing."

Now what should you do? You could wait for Ki, but who knows if he'll return? If you don't want to wait, you could buy a map and go look for temples yourself.

If you decide to wait to see if Ki comes back, turn to page 112.

If you decide to leave now and continue the search alone, turn to page 107.

98

You thank the old man profusely and make a generous contribution to the temple's rebuilding fund. Then you head off to find an inn to spend the night. Leaving your backpack there, you return to the temple at five as planned.

Ki appears to be a rather stern, silent type. He answers your questions briefly, or not at all, and seems not to be too pleased with his new job. But you decide to make the best of it. There have already been enough delays. You don't have time to look for a more enjoyable companion.

Turn to page 92.

As soon as your feet are free, you kick the servant in the knee and dash down the staircase. You make it halfway across the yard before a shot rings out and hits you in the neck.

Mr. Sing has just enough time to drag your body into the bushes before a worried neighbor comes to his front gate.

"It was just an intruder," Mr. Sing assures him. "I fired a shot into the air. It's the best way to scare off those types."

The next day your body is driven down to Mr. Sing's beach house. Two of Mr. Sing's henchmen throw your body into the Gulf of Thailand. It's no coincidence that the title of Sen Sing's next mystery is The Unwanted Body.

The End

"The monk brought me back to his monastery, where he and the other monks nursed me carefully to health," Thompson continues. "At first I was quite lonely for my old life back in Bangkok. But as I observed the monks, as I watched their calm and simple lives, the silk business looked more and more foolish to me. There was something so hopeless and impermanent about the parties and business deals and travels. Back in my old life I had grown to love Buddhist art, but here I learned to love the life that inspired it. By the time I was well enough to return, I didn't want to anymore. Fate had handed me a chance to start over. I took it. I became a monk like the others. Today and every day I beg, meditate, heal, and teach. I am nothing now," he says smiling.

"But what will everyone say when they find out?" you blurt.

Jim Thompson rises. "They never will if you don't tell them," he says. Then he bows, nods and walks off into the jungle.

Turn to page 113.

At dawn you wake up suddenly. Standing on the dock is an old man dressed in monks' robes.

"Wh . . . wh . . . who are you?" you stutter in a frightened voice.

But the next thing you know, he's vanished. You jump up. "Wait!" you yell, running down the dock toward the jungle. "Where did you go?"

You stumble around the jungle, but you can't find the monk anywhere. Half an hour later, you return to the boat.

"Where were you?" asks Ning, rubbing her eyes.

"I saw a monk here. He was standing right next to the boat," you tell her. "Then he just disappeared! I looked for him in the jungle, but all I found were mosquitoes," you add, scratching.

"You were probably dreaming," Ning says. "Let's get going."

You travel on to Ayutthaya and spend a week searching for Thompson, with no luck. You decide to return to Bangkok, but on the night before you leave, you wake up with a fever and chills. The next day a doctor diagnoses a case of malaria, probably caught from the mosquitoes in the bird sanctuary.

It's off to the hospital with you. Your search for Thompson is finished.

The End

Quietly, so that you don't wake Ning, you climb out of the boat and crouch on the dock, staring into the forest. The light flashes again. This time you begin walking toward it.

You go along a high path, with what appears to be a marsh on either side. The light is coming from much farther off than you thought. As you get closer, you can see that it's coming from a broken-down stone building nestled among a clutch of ancient trees. You move silently along the front of the building. But when you turn the corner, you are unprepared for what you see.

"Mr. Thompson?" you gasp, falling to your knees.

The old monk who sits meditating before you calmly raises his head. When he opens his eyes, you become sure that the man is Thompson.

At first you're afraid he's not going to say anything. But after a few seconds he begins to speak.

Turn to page 93.

104

Along with several monks staying at the hotel, you start walking through the flooded streets toward the high ground across the flood plain. You try carrying your pack, but you need every ounce of strength to fight the raging water and keep your balance. Removing your passport, tickets, and papers, you throw the pack off and watch it float away.

It seems to take forever to reach the high ground. Actually only ten minutes pass before you arrive at a small outlying village crowded with refugees like yourself. The village turns out to be the site of a thriving silk manufacturing business. You're stranded there for several days, so you have the chance to find out a good deal about the village's history.

Turn to page 110.

Unfortunately, the celebrations are premature. A routine dental identification proves that the skeleton isn't Jim Thompson's at all. Doctors think that it's actually the skeleton of one of the aborigines who live in the Cameron Highlands. He must have found Thompson's watch in the jungle. Still, that doesn't necessarily mean Thompson is dead.

In the meantime, the monk in the photographs remains unfound, and your money runs out. When you board your return flight to the United States a few days later, no one even gives you a second glance.

The End

106

Your rescue boat is weighed down badly, and the driver has difficulty navigating. An old man carries a squawking chicken under his arm. Another carries a sack filled with what appears to be his entire earthly possessions, including a small table and chair. Your boat turns around the corner of some buildings and starts across the flood plain. The water rushes past violently, and the boat lists dangerously to one side.

Someone yells, "The boat is leaking!"

Several people scream and stand up all at once. It's just enough to tip the boat. You are flung along with the rest into the muddy, raging water. Your pack is ripped out of your hands by the surging water.

You fight valiantly and manage to keep your head above water until some mysterious object floats by. It bonks you in the head, and you're knocked out cold.

Turn to page 7.

"The heck with waiting for Ki," you mumble aloud, gathering up your gear. You pay your bill and head out into the rain. At the local store you buy a map with jungle trails marked. The storekeeper helps you to plot the way to the closest temple, and you set off.

The map turns out to be fairly accurate, and you find the first temple without any trouble. Unfortunately, the monks have no information about Thompson. They do point out on your map the way to the next monastery, though. On your way you feel confident enough to veer off the trail a bit to examine a beautiful butterfly that flutters past you and lands in a nearby tree. As you walk toward it, you feel sharp stinging pricks in your leg.

You've stepped on a wild hornets' nest. They're stinging you all over!

Turn to page 111.

108

In silent agreement, you and Ki begin climbing the stairs. You are awestruck by the size of some of the foundation stones. The temple is built in stories, and each seems even more beautiful than the last. When you get to the topmost sanctuary, Ki tells you, "This is the temple in honor of the god Siva."

Suddenly a voice barks, "And this is where you've gone too far."

Three machine gun-toting men wearing red scarves step around the corner. You turn to run, but several others have blocked the stairs.

"This must be a Khmer Rouge hideout," Ki whispers, stricken. "We're in for it now."

The End

You dash up to your room, grab your backpack, and hurry toward the train station with most of the others staying at the hotel. People stream from every direction, nervous and rushed. Soon the road is packed. In the crunch, an old monk walking near you gets knocked over. He struggles to get up, but in the confusion, no one else seems to notice. You reach over to help. Finally, you carry him piggyback the rest of the way.

When you arrive, the train station is swarming with people. It looks as if you will have a long wait; there are only a few rescue boats. But the monk you have been carrying turns out to be of some importance. He is dispatched in one of the next boats, and he insists that you be taken, too.

Turn to page 106.

For a long while, you learn, the village was extremely poor. Ten years ago some monks arrived and taught the villagers how to raise silkworms on the surrounding mulberry trees. Then the monks taught them how to make silk thread and weave it into fabric. They explained dye techniques. One of the monks, who knew more than the rest, even helped design patterns for the fabric.

"And he wasn't even Thai!" someone exclaims.

Excitedly you pull the faded news clipping about Thompson from your pocket.

"This man?" you ask, pointing to the picture.

Several people nod excitedly. One man says, "That monk left our village after the silk business was running smoothly. He has never returned, but if he did, he would get the welcome of a saint!"

The End

You fling your pack down and run wildly through the jungle. Up ahead you spot a stream, and not a moment too soon. In seconds the hornets would have stung you to death. You dive in.

You lie in the cool stream till the hornets have disappeared. But by then your body has swollen up so much it's hard to move. Luckily for you, Ki has come after you. He arrives a few minutes later. Seeing you in the stream, he bursts out laughing. You're embarrassed, but worse, you're in serious pain. It's no laughing matter. You're going to spend time in the local hospital to clear out the poisons and it means your search is over.

The End

112

You wait just inside the inn, watching the doorway. A half hour later Ki appears.

"Ki, where were you?" you cry.

But instead of answering your question, he says, "No guerrillas in sight. It will be safe to search temples close to the border."

"How far exactly are we from Cambodia?" you ask.

"About thirty-five kilometers," Ki answers. "Today we go part way by jeep."

"Okay," you say weakly, trying to hide your nervousness.

Through the inn, you arrange to hire a jeep with driver and start out. Around lunchtime you hit pay dirt. One of the monks at the fourth temple you stop at thinks he has seen Thompson before, perhaps a year ago.

"Yes, he is connected with a forest temple here," he adds, drawing a map for Ki in the mud.

Ki directs your driver toward the spot. Soon the jeep stops in the middle of nowhere and Ki hops out. "We walk the rest of the way from here."

"Isn't it getting late to be heading into the jungle?" you ask nervously.

Ki looks at you in disgust. "Do you want to find this monk or not?" he answers gruffly. Then, he strides forward into the jungle.

"I do, I do!" you say quickly, running after him.

Turn to page 115.

You return slowly to the dock. Sitting there, you think about Jim Thompson's amazing life till the sun starts to rise. You almost wonder if you've been dreaming.

Ning shifts in the boat and sits up. "Time to begin the search for Thompson?" she asks in a sleepy voice.

"I don't think so," you reply.

"What?" Ning says, waking up now. "You don't want to search for Thompson anymore?"

You shrug. "I've got a feeling that the Jim Thompson we're all looking for no longer exists," you reply. And you think to yourself, *if he does still exist, he's made his choice how to lead his life, and therefore, it's better to respect that.*

The End

The trail you follow winds back and forth up a hill. Ki seems excited at last. He darts through the heavy undergrowth quickly. Monsoon clouds cover the sky, but you can tell by the fading light that it's getting late.

Finally, you emerge from the jungle. Before you, a magnificent old temple stands at the edge of a cliff. It must be a half-mile long. Awesome stairs lead up through succeeding stories marked by huge, elaborate archways. Every surface is covered with the weathered remains of intricate carving.

"What is it?" you ask.

"Khao Phra Viharn," Ki announces, breaking into his first smile of the day as he points at the incredible structure. "Those stairs are supposed to lead to heaven."

Turn to page 108.

116

"Ning, Ning!" you whisper, shaking your friend gently. "Wake up!"

"Wha . . . what? What? Is that you?" she says sleepily.

"Yes. Ning, I just had this weird dream," you say. "I dreamt that I was walking through the jungle and I came to this big house. I went inside and my grandmother was there. She told me I was looking for Thompson in the wrong place. She said, 'Thompson is near the river, not the mountains.' But when I asked her what river, she wouldn't tell me."

Ning sits up, rubbing her eyes, and asks, "Is your grandmother dead or alive?"

"You mean in real life? She's dead. She died a year ago," you answer. "Why?"

"According to Thai beliefs," Ning explains, "if you dream about someone who is alive, it usually only reflects some aspect of your relationship with that person. But if a person you dream about, especially a relative, is dead, it means that that person's spirit has actually come to help you. Your grandmother visited you in your dream on purpose. She knows something we don't! We will leave first thing in the morning. It would be bad luck to ignore such advice."

Turn to page 63.

CREDITS

Interior illustrators:
Thananart Kornmaneeroj (Yo). Thananart was born in Chantaburi, Thailand. In addition to his artistic endeavors, he is an architect and a lecturer in the Department of Architecture at Chulalongkorn University.

Kachaine Chanchareon (Chaine). Kachaine is from Pra Juab Kirikan, Thailand. Kachaine works for Ayutthaya Building Co. Ltd. His drawings are enhanced by his experience in traditional Thai architecture.

Sorasith Butsingkhon (Kai). Sorasith was born in Roi Ed, Thailand and works for Geoartfact in Bangkok, Thailand.

Atthakrit Utahigarn (Note). Atthakrit hails from Prayao, Thailand and is a freelance artist with an architectural background.

Cover Illustrator: Jose Luis Marron lives and works in Madrid. He has studied film at universities in Canada and France. Jose worked for several years in the Spanish film and television industry, before turning to design and illustration full-time. He has illustrated seven *Choose Your Own Adventure®* covers.

This book was brought to life by a great group of people:

Shannon Gilligan, Publisher
Gordon Troy, General Counsel
Jason Gellar, Sales Director
Melissa Bounty, Senior Editor
Stacey Boyd, Designer

Thanks to everyone involved!

ABOUT THE AUTHOR

SHANNON GILLIGAN is a well-known creator of interactive narrative games for the computer. She has spoken about interactive narrative and game design at conferences in Japan, Europe and the United States. Gilligan got her start in this field by writing for the *Choose Your Own Adventure*® series in the 1980s. Her books and games have sold several million copies around the world. She graduated from Williams College in 1981 and lives in Warren, Vermont with her husband R. A. Montgomery and her extended family. She returns to Asia at least once a year. Gilligan harbors a secret ambition to write a cookbook.

For games, activities and other fun stuff, or to write to Shannon Gilligan, visit us online at CYOA.com

ADVENTURER'S LOG

ADVENTURER'S LOG

ADVENTURER'S LOG

ADVENTURER'S LOG

ADVENTURER'S LOG

ADVENTURER'S LOG

ADVENTURER'S LOG

ADVENTURER'S LOG

ADVENTURER'S LOG

ADVENTURER'S LOG

ADVENTURER'S LOG

Original Fans Love Reading
Choose Your Own Adventure®!

The books let readers remix their own stories—and face the consequences. Kids race to discover lost civilizations, navigate black holes, and go in search of the Yeti, revamped for the 21st century!
Wired Magazine

I love CYOA—I missed CYOA! I've been keeping my fingers as bookmarks on pages 45, 16, 32, and 9 all these years, just to keep my options open.
Madeline, 20

Reading a CYOA book was more like playing a video game on my treasured Nintendo® system. I'm pretty sure the multiple plot twists of *The Lost Jewels of Nabooti* are forever stored in some part of my brain.
The Fort Worth Star Telegram

How I miss you, CYOA! I only have a small shelf left after my mom threw a bunch of you away in a yard sale—she never did understand.
Travis Rex, 26

I LOVE CYOA BOOKS! I have read them since I was a small child. I am so glad to hear they are going back into print! You have just made me the happiest person in the world!
Carey Walker, 27

Silk King Trivia Quiz

The Silk King is an elusive case.
Prove your investigative skills, or return
to the case for a little more sleuthing.

1) **What is in the mysterious envelope you open at the very start of your adventure?**
   A. Nothing
   B. Two feathers, a compass, and a map
   C. A letter
   D. Two one-thousand dollar bills, a plane ticket, and a newspaper article

2) **Who is the "Thai Silk King"?**
   A. Sam, your secretary
   B. Jim Thompson
   C. You have no idea
   D. John Atwood

3) **What does OSS stand for?**
   A. Operation Standard Service
   B. Old Slimy Slugs
   C. Office of Shooting Stars
   D. Office of Strategic Services

4) **Who is Ning Thanon?**
   A. The Silk King
   B. A Thai exchange student, whom you befriended
   C. The person who sent you the tickets and the money
   D. A Buddhist monk

5) **What are Pedicabs?**
   A. A kind of bicycle rickshaw
   B. A kind of boat
   C. A kind of noodle
   D. A cross between a pedicure and a cab

6) **What is the name of the resort in Malaysia that Jim Thompson disappeared from?**
   A. Holiday Inn Express
   B. Malaysialand
   C. Cameron Highlands
   D. Cameroon Lowlands

7) **Who visits you in a creepy dream you have in Malaysia.**
   A. Your uncle
   B. Your cousin
   C. Your father
   D. Your grandmother

8) **Where does your grandmother tell you to look in your dream?**
   A. The hotel
   B. The river
   C. The Great Valley
   D. China

9) **What object with Jim Thompson's initials on it is found on a skeleton?**
   A. A handkerchief
   B. A ring
   C. A watch
   D. A pair of pants

9) **What has Mr. Thompson become?**
   A. A profession wrestler
   B. A garbage man
   C. A monkey
   D. A monk

THE GOLDEN PATH

ARE YOU READY?

SEVEN BOOK INTERACTIVE EPIC

FOR AGES 12+

INTEGRATED COLLECTABLE CARD GAME